Love Poems

for

Mary

STEPHEN PEREZ

I0617113

Love Poems for Mary
Copyright © 2022 by Stephen Perez

ISBN
978-1-957895-60-4 (Paperback)
978-1-957895-61-1 (eBook)

TABLE OF CONTENTS

THE OWNER OF MY HEART

You are the owner of my heart

You own me heart and soul.

I was lonely and dead inside

With no true emotions to show.

Then you came into my life

And you filled the empty hole.

You put a spark back in my heart

Filled with love and so much more.

You showed me I could love again

And that life can truly be sweet.

My love for you is strong and true.

And it grows with each passing week.

You told me that you don't want

Anything serious, and my love

might all be in vain.

But I will love you anyway

And gladly take the pain.

The pain will be hard and it will

Be deep.

But the memories I have made will

Still be just as sweet.

He brought you into my life and

For that I thank God every day.

So if it is his will, in my life

Is where you will stay.

If things don't work out and we

Still have to part,

Please just know one thing

You are the owner of my heart.

A
CHRISTMAS
WISH

Christmas is my favorite time

Of year.

It's when people are friendlier,

Warmer and more caring.

It's when children of all ages

Get their wishes granted

A time when parents can count

Their blessings.

A Christmas wish is a special one

A wish that is blessed from above,

My wish this Christmas season is

That you open your heart

And capture all my love.

It's a magical time of year

When dreams can and do come true.

A time to make special memories

Of loving moments spent with you.

Relationships are special this time of year

Somehow they seem to flourish.

All of this can happen

With one little Christmas wish.

THIS
PERSON

This person, this amazing person

That always drives me crazy.

This person, that doesn't know she

Is beautiful.

She never ceases to amaze me.

This person, that never tells me that

She loves me.

Somehow always lets me know.

She really does love and care for me

But never lets it show.

This person, that holds my heart in her hands

She means the world to me.

If only she would let me into her life

How Happy I would be.

This person that turns my world upside

Down, and if she only knew.

How much I really need her

This amazing person is you.

OUR FIRST KISS

13

The first time we kissed was magic

I didn't want the moment to end.

My head was all a Flutter

The whole night went by like a whirlwind.

Each time we kiss I fall deeper

And I hope I never come out.

My feelings for you grow stronger

To the whole world I want to shout.

My life would be so much brighter

If only you would open your heart.

Give my love a little chance.

That would be such a great start.

Let's get our life started together

Time is slipping away.

If you would only let me love you

That would really make my whole day.

A Day Without You

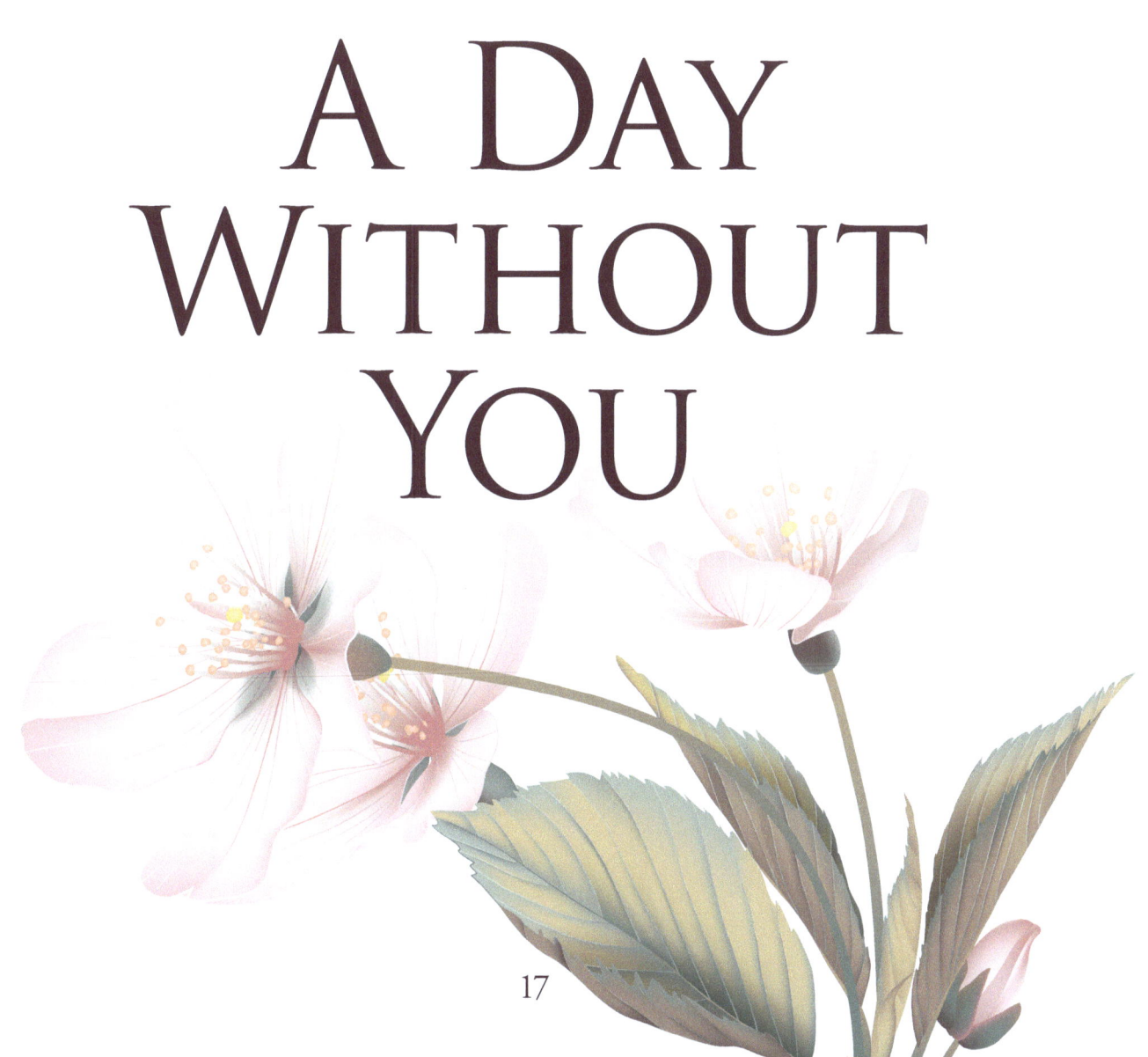

A day without you is like

A day without air.

I love everything about you

From your toes to your hair.

I can't imagine an hour without you

Much less a whole day.

That's like having a pain

That won't go away.

I love you; I need you

Of that there is no doubt.

With your love and your caring

I can't do without.

I wait till the day

That you wake in my arms.

A day of renewed love And life in my heart.

How Do I Love Thee

I love it when you lean over the

Counter to check your phone.

I love it when you wrinkle your nose

When you say certain things.

I love the view when you're walking toward me.

I love the view when you're walking away.

I love the different ways you wear your hair.

I love the way you move when you walk.

I love the way you wave when you say goodbye.

I love the way you make me feel

When I'm with you.

I definitely love your hugs and kisses

These are just a few little things I love about you.

"tu eres mi vida y te amo con todo

Mi Corazon."

Translation:

"You are my life and

I love you with all my heart."

MY
PROMISE

I promise I will never

Hurt you, and I will never

Make you cry.

I promise to never make

You doubt my love, and

To never make you ask why.

I promise that I will love

You forever, and work to make

All your dreams come true.

I promise to keep you in

Mind in everything I do.

I promise that you are my

Only one, and I will never stray

There is no one else I could

Ever love this way.

I promise that I will take care

Of you, and never take you for granted.

I can promise all of this because

You're everything I've wanted.

ON THE WINGS OF YOUR LOVE

Riding on the wings of your love

I start to face another day.

With your love in my heart

There is nothing I can't face.

The world can be a scary place. With

So much going on.

I just get lost in you and all

My worries are gone.

When I'm with you, you're the

Only one I see.

There is no place I would rather be.

You make my life complete, you

Are my world.

You are my everything, without

You, I would be lost.

HAPPINESS

Happiness is being with the one

You love, and spending

Time together.

Never wanting the moment to

End, to be with you forever.

Happiness is seeing your smiling

Face every day, and making

Special memories.

It goes a long way to brighten

My day, and it makes me very Happy.

Happiness is wanting to spend our

Days together.

Being side by side From now until

Forever.

Happiness is wanting to hold and love

You. Never wanting to part.

You're always on my mind

You're always in my heart.

WHEN IT COMES TO YOU

When it comes to you, I am the

Biggest fool in town.

Like a little puppy, I follow you

All around.

When it comes to you, my love

Will never die.

You're like a drug to me and you

Always keep me high.

When it comes to you, my feelings

All go crazy.

I can't even think straight

Everything goes hazy.

I'll be there to share with you

All you say and do.

I'll be there, when it comes to you.

I
NEED
YOU

I need you like the flowers

Need rain.

You're like a breath of fresh air.

You brighten my day

You make my heart aware.

I need you like romance needs

The moon.

You're everything to me.

Time stands still when I'm with you

There is no one with whom I would

Rather be.

I need you like I need air

To breathe.

I can't see my life without you.

You're all I ever think about

You're there in everything I do.

I need you in my life

Like a kite needs the wind.

I will always love you

From now until the end.

MY SENSES

You make my senses come alive

You wake them up all five.

I love to watch you as you move

Here and there.

To me there is no other sight that

Can compare.

I love to listen to the sound of your voice

Whenever I hear it, it makes me rejoice.

I love the taste of your lips,

They bring me joy.

They make me realize that I am

A very lucky boy.

I love the smell of your hair as

I lean in to kiss you.

It smells like flowers in the

Morning dew.

I love the feel of your skin next to mine

It's as intoxicating as a glass of wine.

www.ingramcontent.com/pod-product-compliance
Lightning Source LLC
Chambersburg PA
CBHW041554120626
46551CB00002B/200